Fierce Jobs
Search and Rescue

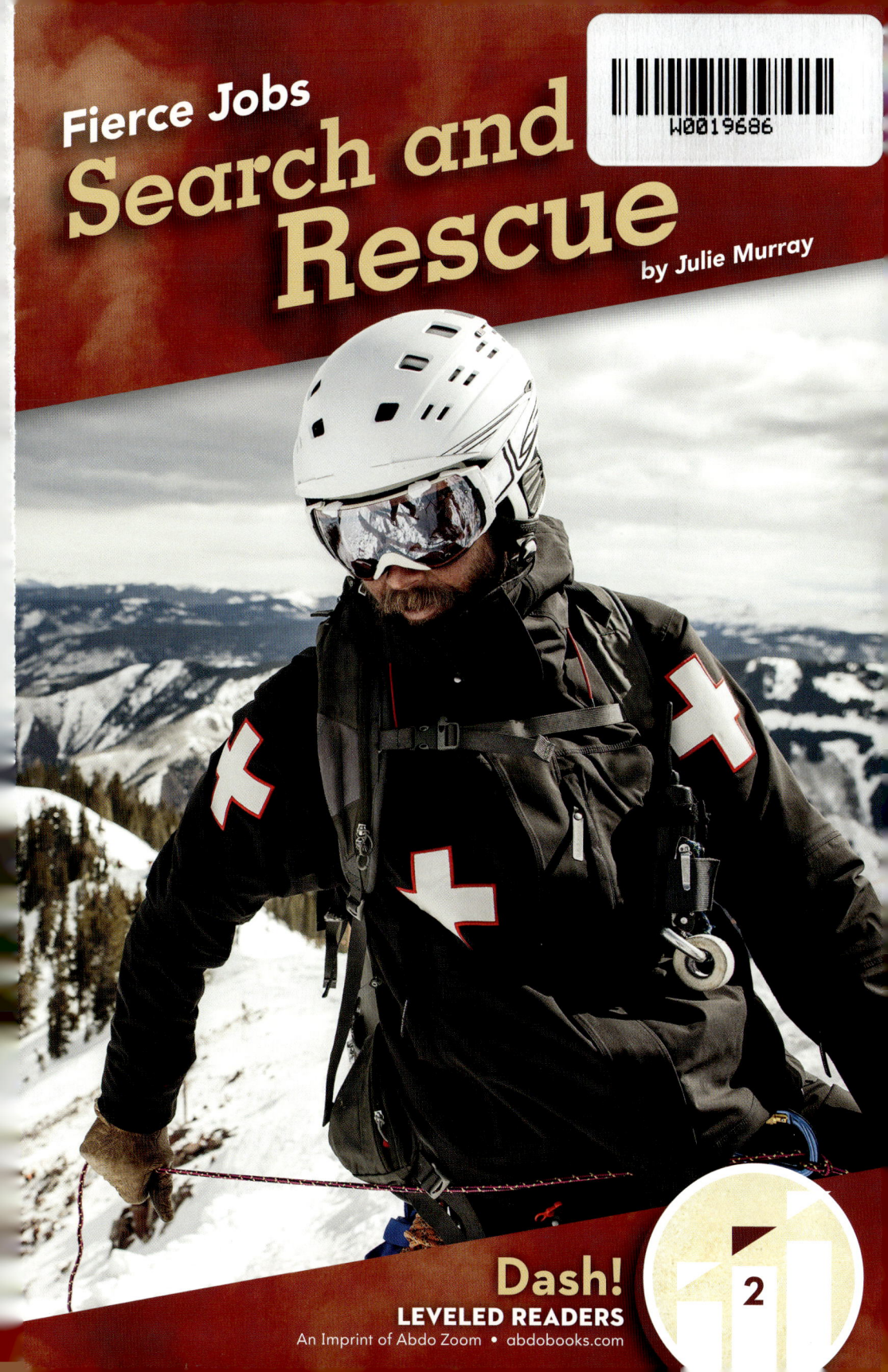

by Julie Murray

Dash!
LEVELED READERS
An Imprint of Abdo Zoom • abdobooks.com

2

Dash!
LEVELED READERS

Level 1 – Beginning
Short and simple sentences with familiar words or patterns for children who are beginning to understand how letters and sounds go together.

Level 2 – Emerging
Longer words and sentences with more complex language patterns for readers who are practicing common words and letter sounds.

Level 3 – Transitional
More developed language and vocabulary for readers who are becoming more independent.

THIS BOOK CONTAINS RECYCLED MATERIALS

abdobooks.com

Published by Abdo Zoom, a division of ABDO, PO Box 398166, Minneapolis, Minnesota 55439.
Copyright © 2021 by Abdo Consulting Group, Inc. International copyrights reserved in all countries. No part of this book may be reproduced in any form without written permission from the publisher. Dash!™ is a trademark and logo of Abdo Zoom.

Printed in the United States of America, North Mankato, Minnesota.
052020
092020

Photo Credits: Alamy, Getty Images, iStock, Shutterstock
Production Contributors: Kenny Abdo, Jennie Forsberg, Grace Hansen, John Hansen
Design Contributors: Dorothy Toth, Neil Klinepier, Laura Graphenteen

Library of Congress Control Number: 2019956141

Publisher's Cataloging in Publication Data
Names: Murray, Julie, author.
Title: Search and rescue / by Julie Murray
Description: Minneapolis, Minnesota : Abdo Zoom, 2021 | Series: Fierce jobs | Includes online resources and index.
Identifiers: ISBN 9781098221102 (lib. bdg.) | ISBN 9781644944059 (pbk.) | ISBN 9781098222086 (ebook) | ISBN 9781098222574 (Read-to-Me ebook)
Subjects: LCSH: Search and rescue operations--Juvenile literature. | Rescue work--Juvenile literature. | Lifesaving--Juvenile literature. | Hazardous occupations--Juvenile literature. | Occupations--Juvenile literature.
Classification: DDC 363.1081--dc23

Table of Contents

Search and Rescue. 4

Types of Rescue 8

More Facts 22

Glossary 23

Index 24

Online Resources 24

Search and Rescue

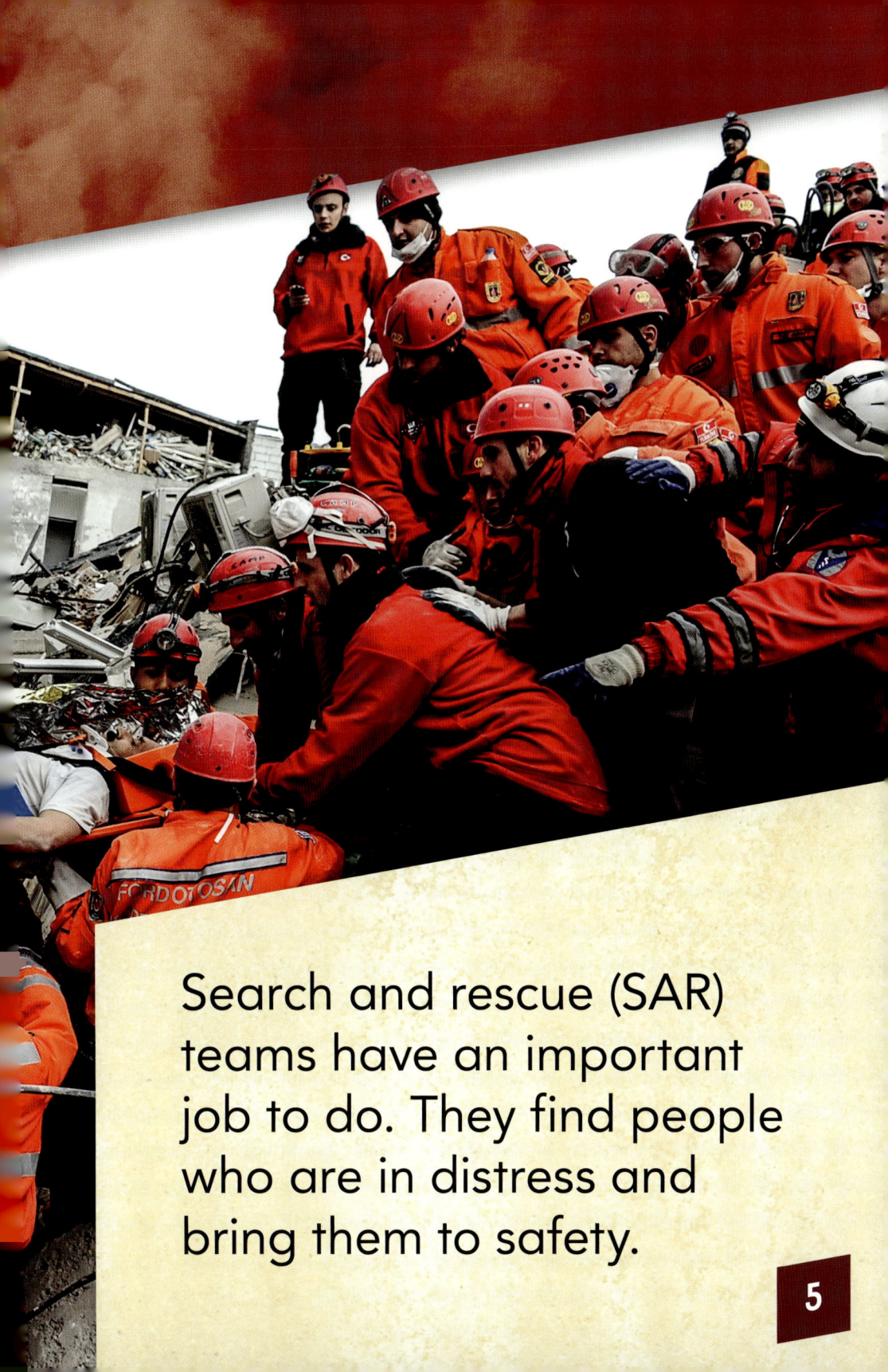

Search and rescue (SAR) teams have an important job to do. They find people who are in distress and bring them to safety.

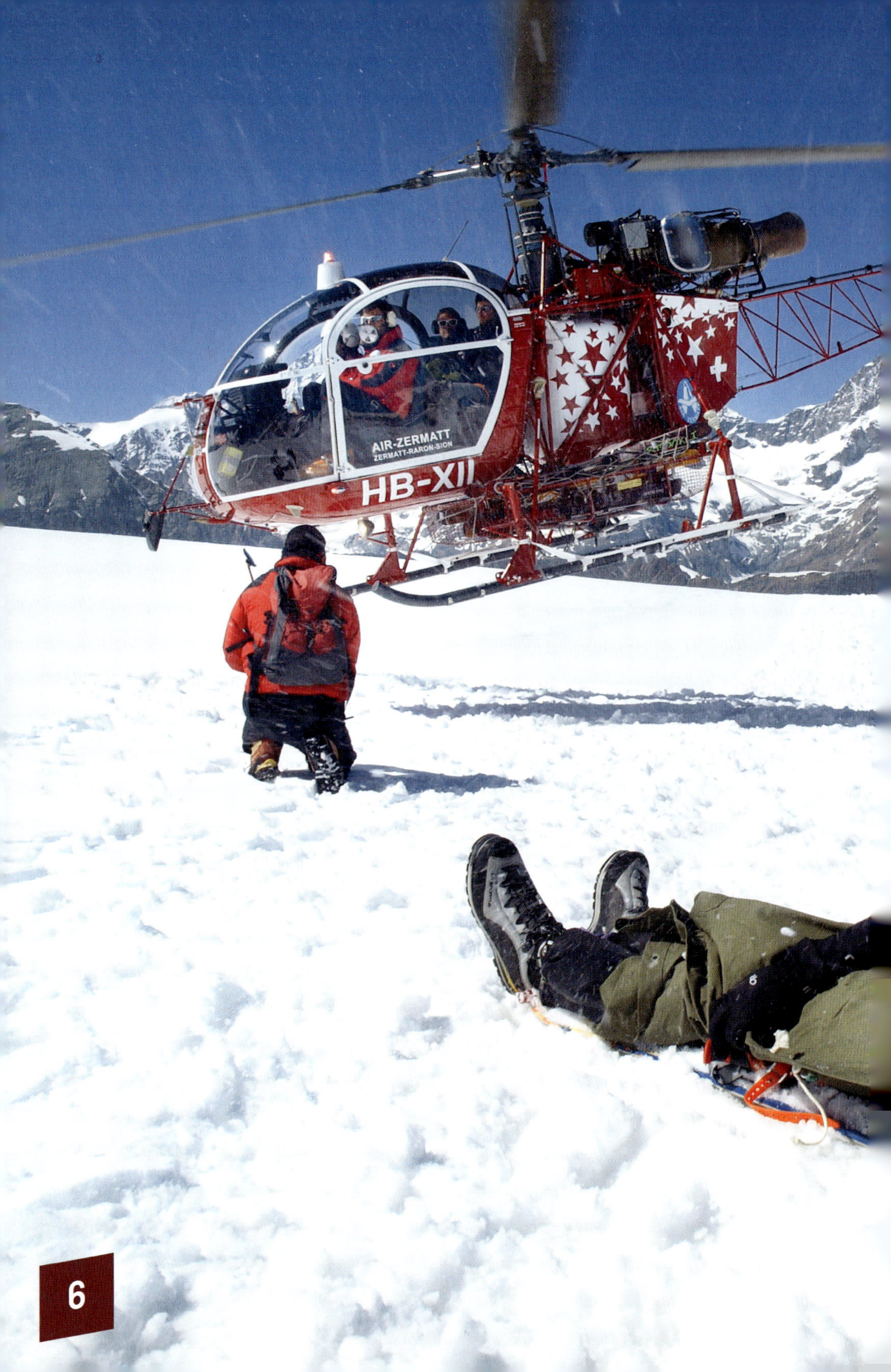
AIR-ZERMATT
ZERMATT-RARON-SION
HB-XII

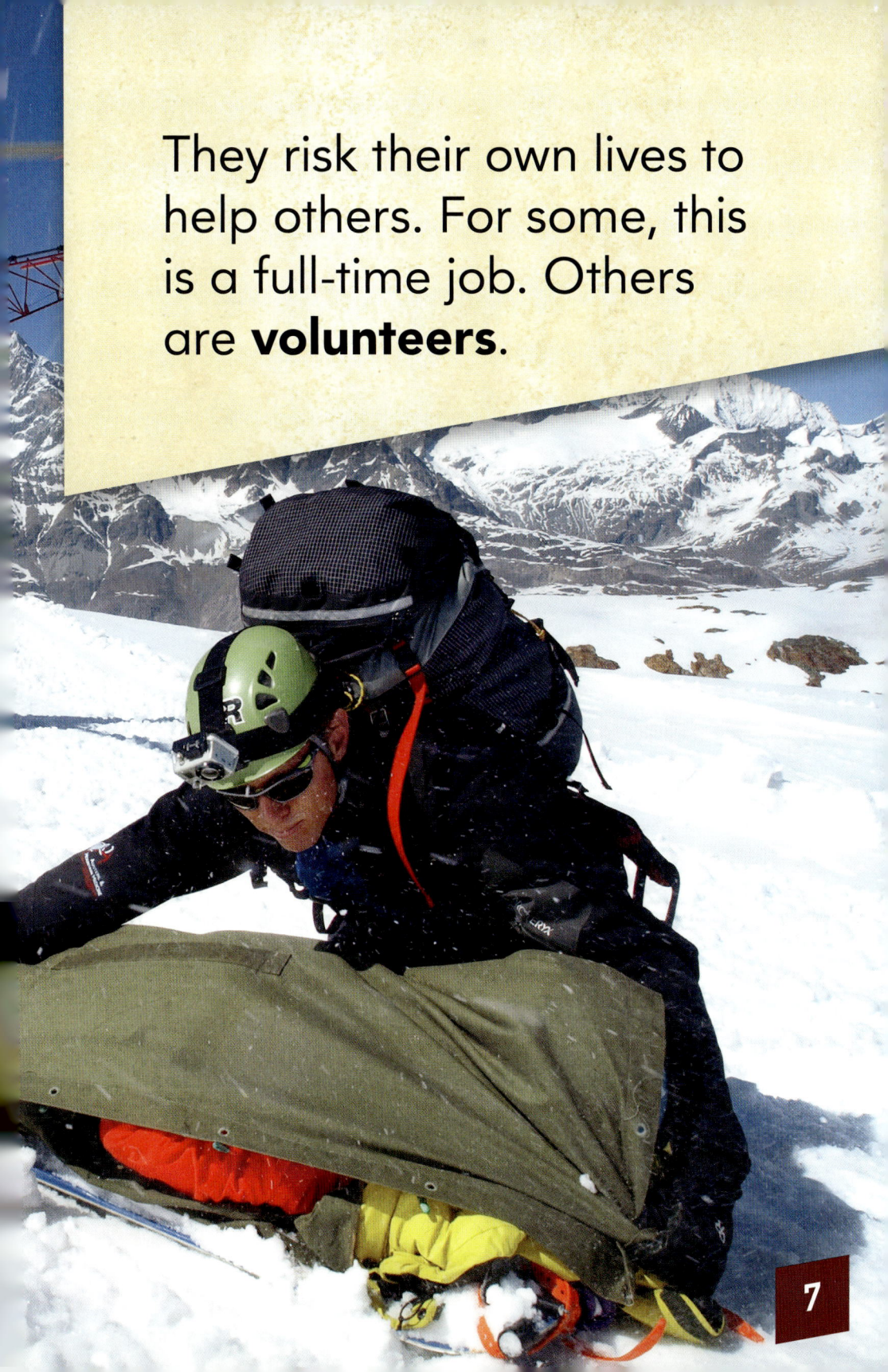

They risk their own lives to help others. For some, this is a full-time job. Others are **volunteers**.

Types of Rescue

SAR teams train on land, air, or water. Some train on all three.

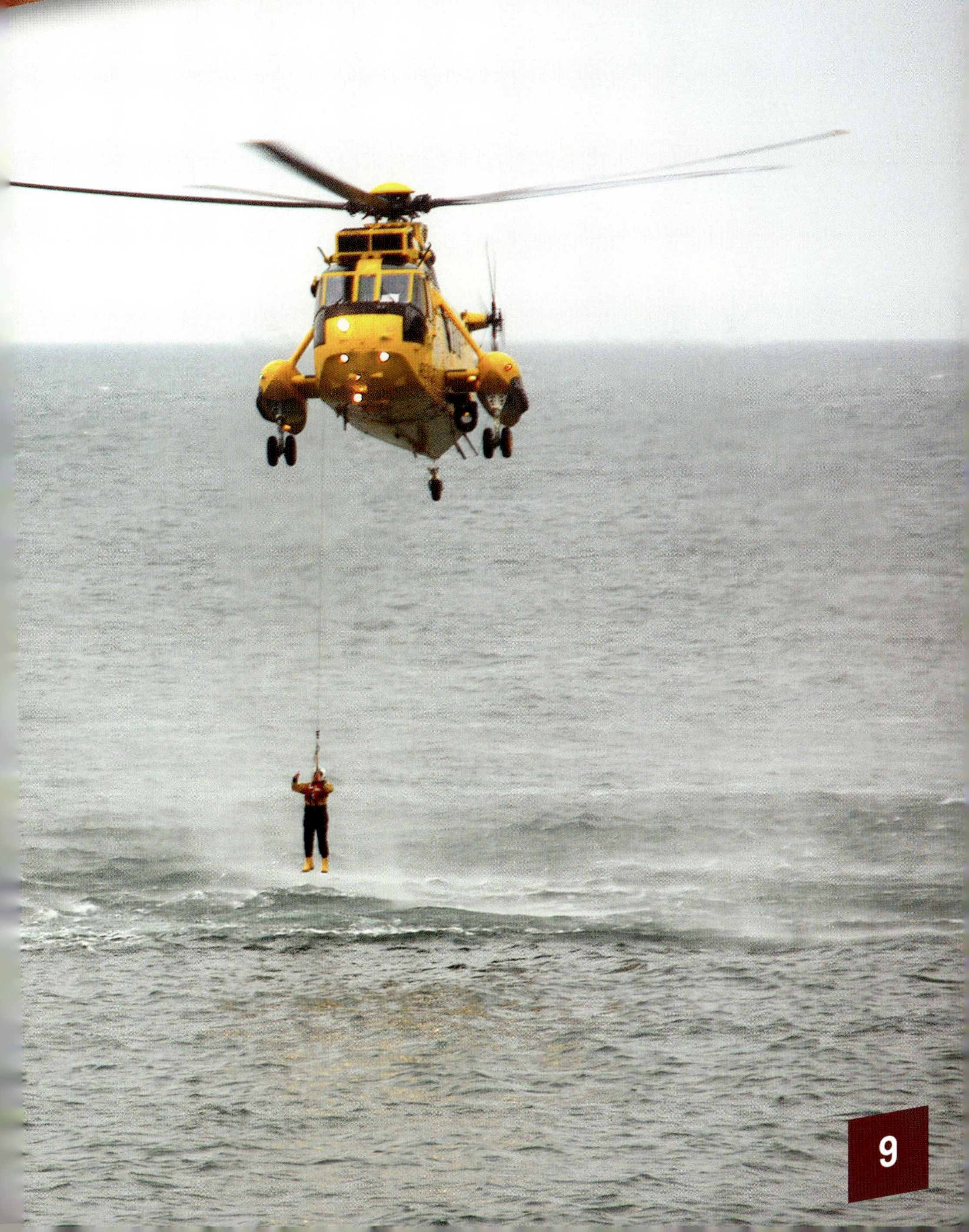

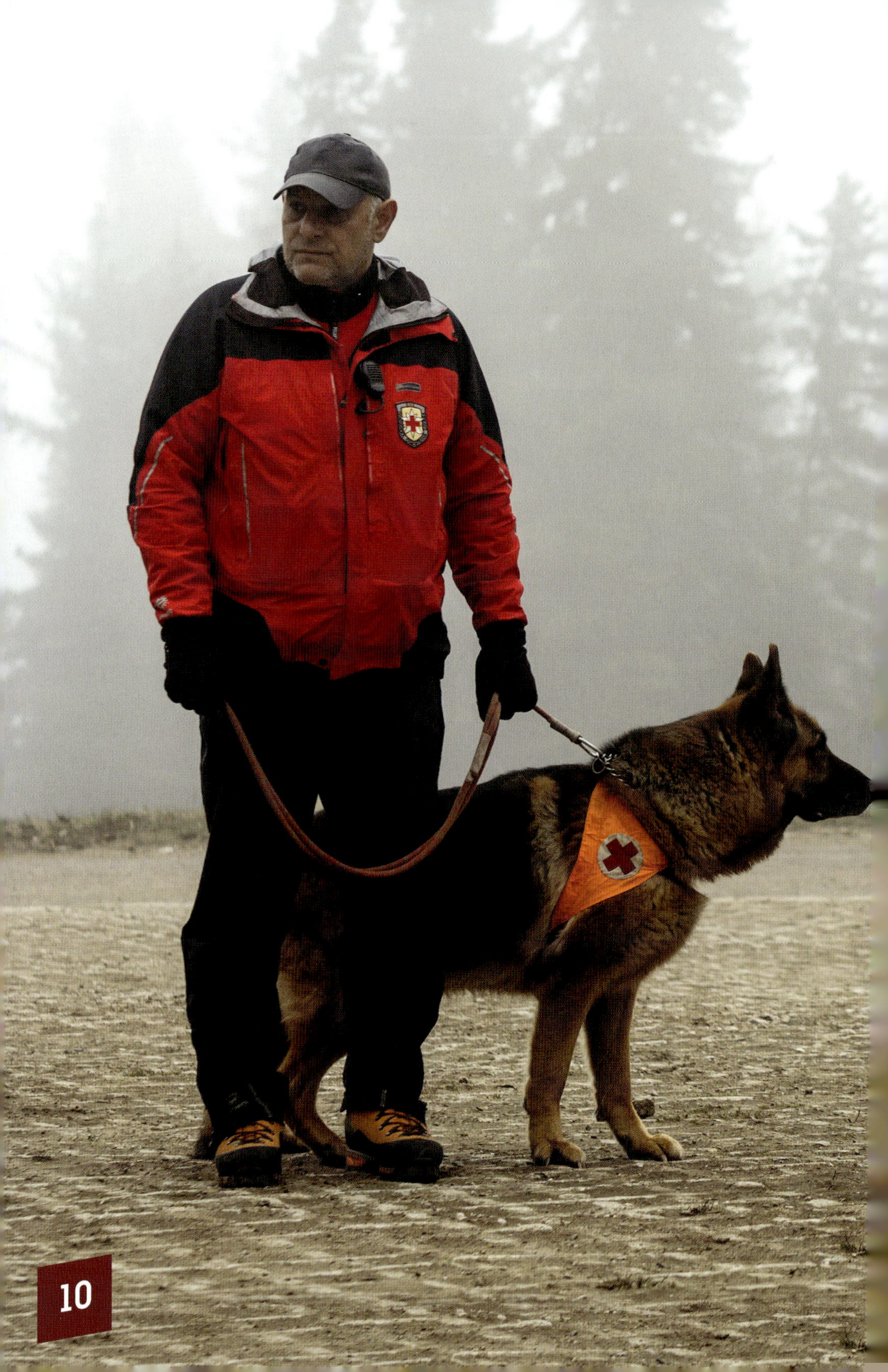

Ground SAR often use dogs. Dogs can easily track a person's scent.

Mountain SAR use dogs too. The pups can pick up a person's scent through deep snow.

13

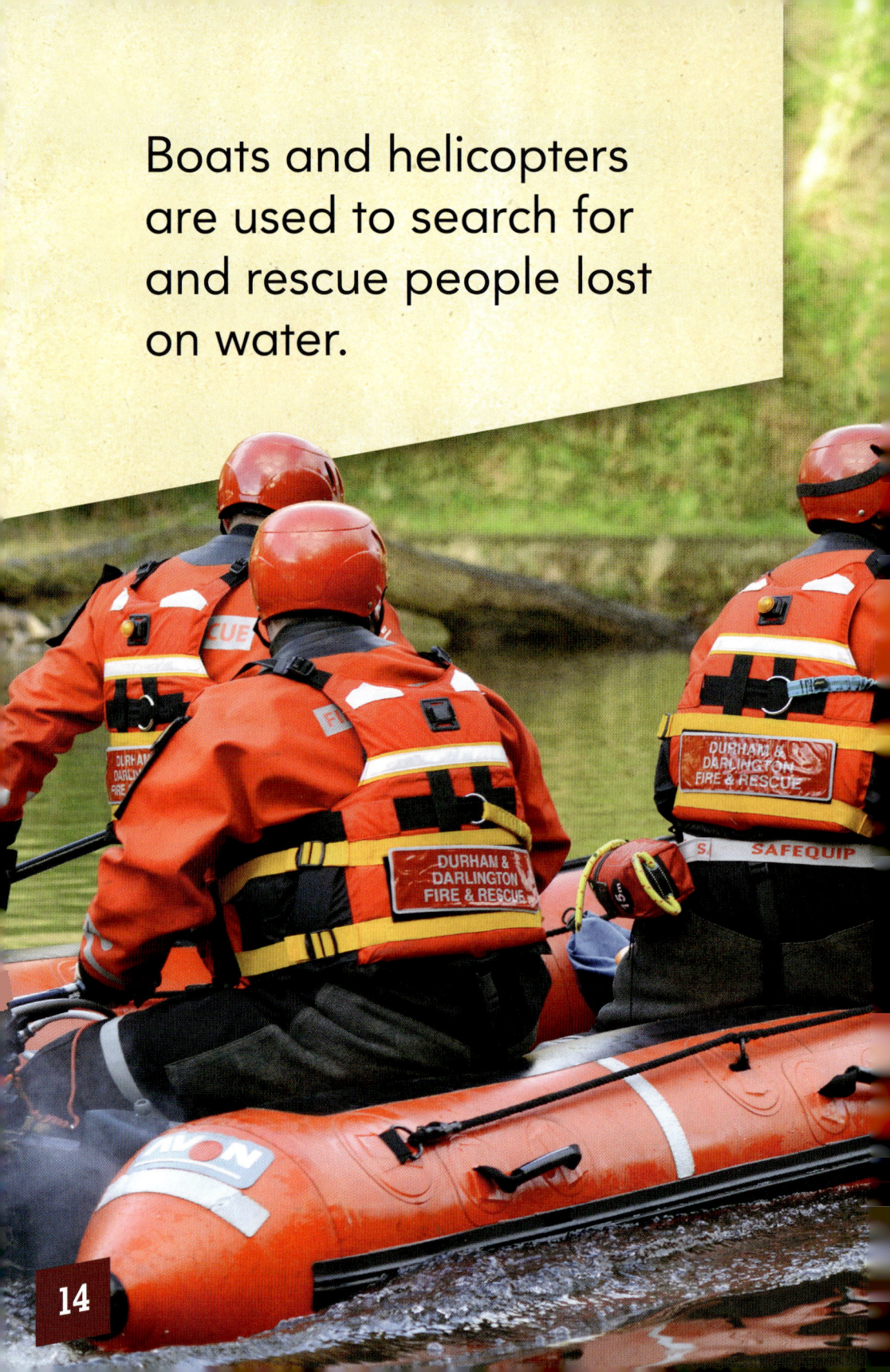

Boats and helicopters are used to search for and rescue people lost on water.

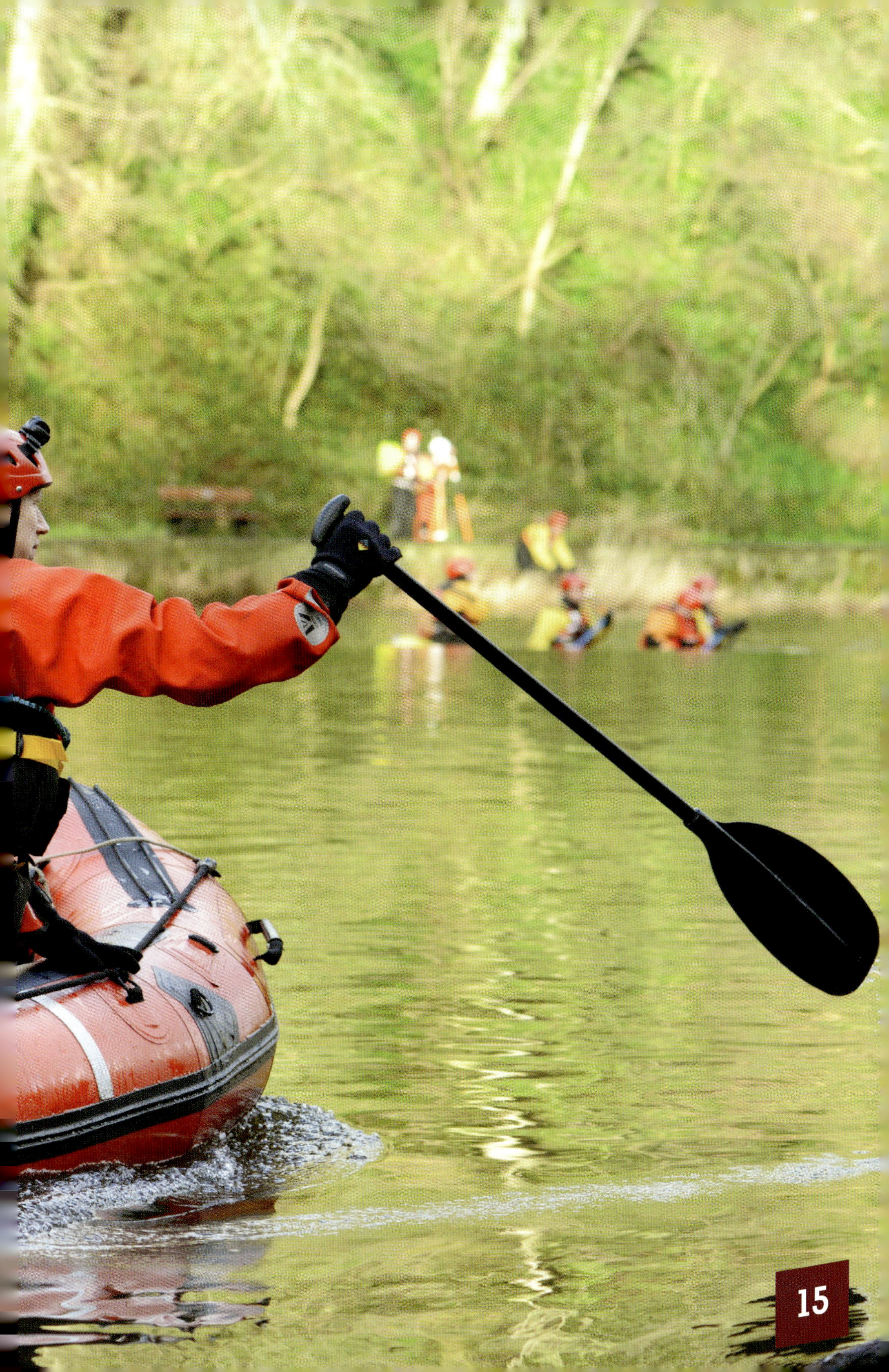

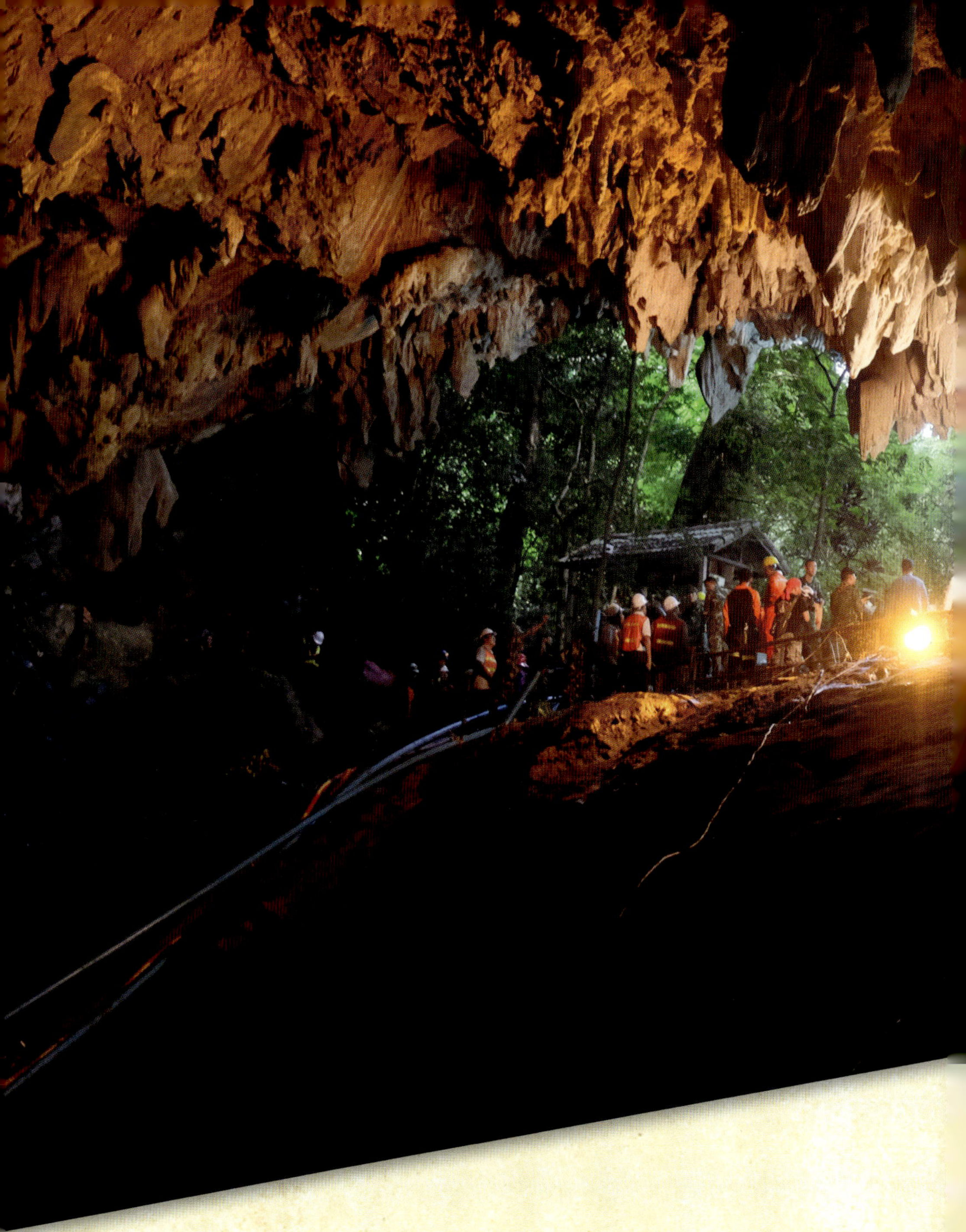

Underground SAR takes place in caves and **mines**. These kinds of rescues need different **specialized** teams.

SAR teams are used after **natural disasters**. They help find people who may be trapped.

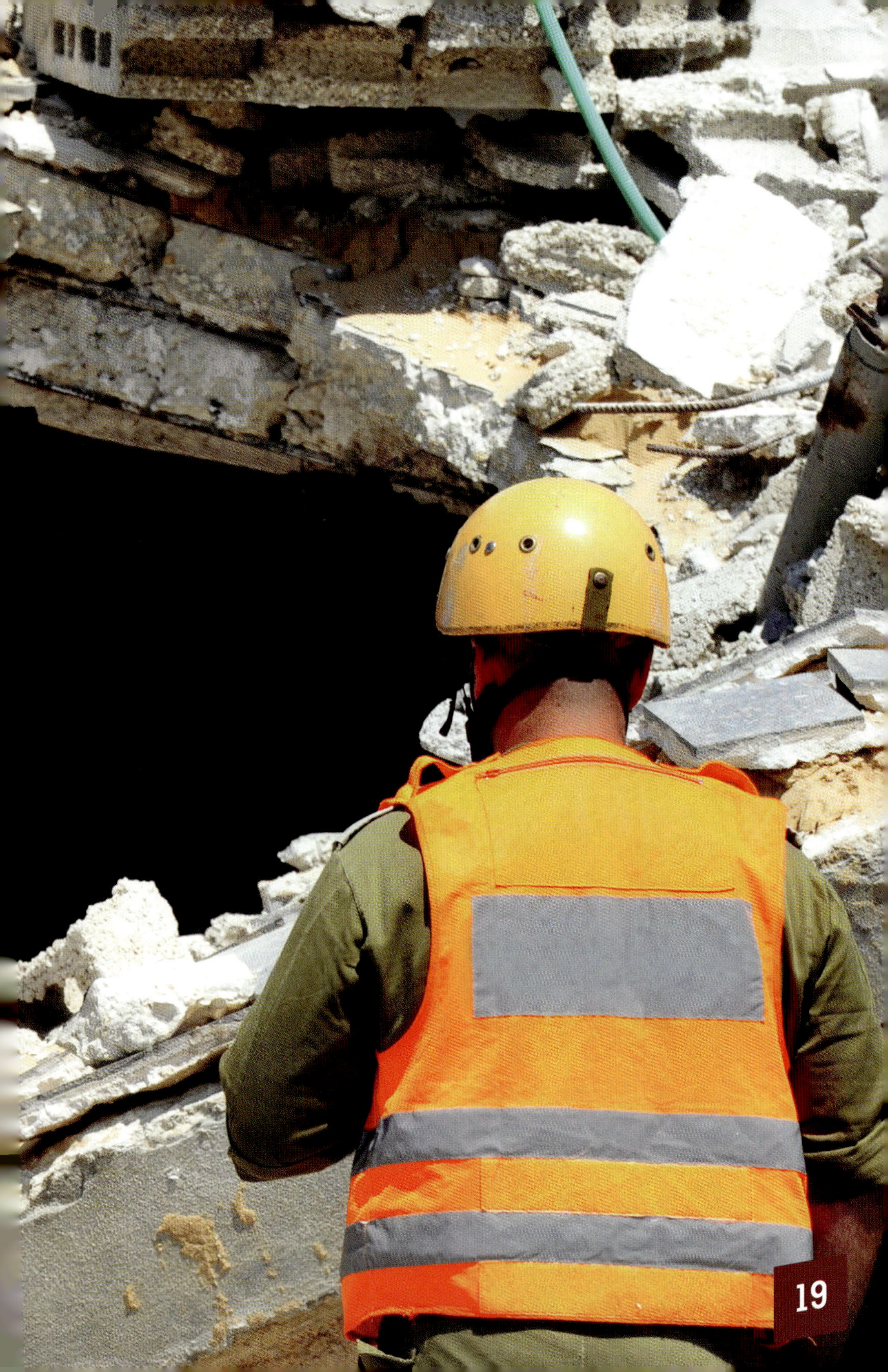

SAR teams are highly trained. They save thousands of lives around the world each year.

21

More Facts

- Search and rescue dogs train for almost two years.

- About 98% of lost people are found alive. Most of them are found within the first 24 hours.

- The US Coast Guard rescues about 115 people each day.

Glossary

mine – a deep hole or area of holes made in the earth where minerals such as gold, coal, or precious stones are dug out of.

natural disaster – a natural event such as a flood, earthquake, or hurricane that causes great damage or loss of life.

specialized – trained for one particular purpose.

volunteer – a person who offers to work or help without pay.

Index

air 8

boats 14

caves 17

dogs 11, 12

helicopter 14

land 8

mines 17

snow 12

training 8, 20

water 8, 14

Online Resources

Booklinks
NONFICTION NETWORK
FREE! ONLINE NONFICTION RESOURCES

To learn more about search and rescue teams, please visit **abdobooklinks.com** or scan this QR code. These links are routinely monitored and updated to provide the most current information available.